Sacred AF

The Spiritual Rebel Guide to Becoming

ORACLE KEYS

Sacred AF: The Spiritual Rebel Guide to Becoming
© 2025 The Khemistry House. All rights reserved.

No part of this book may be reproduced, stored in a retrieval system, or transmitted in any form or by any means — electronic, mechanical, photocopying, recording, or otherwise — without prior written permission of the publisher, except by a reviewer who may quote brief passages in a review.

Published by **The Khemistry House**
An imprint founded by Oracle Keys

ISBN: 979-8-9935932-1-0
Printed in the United States of America

For information, visit: www.thekhemistryhouse.com.

DEDICATION

For Khemistry and Alchemy —
twins of my becoming.
One roots me to earth,
one crowns me in the stars.
Together you are the fire that remade me.

SACRED AF

PREFACE

Spirituality has been dressed up for too long. All white robes, soft voices, and polished edges. Sacred AF is here to burn that illusion down. Because the truth? Spirituality is messy. It's raw. It's holy and profane in the same breath. That's the paradox – and the power.

The title says it plain: Sacred AF. Sacred because your becoming is holy ground. AF because it's not polite, polished, or censored. It's as real as your scars, as raw as your voice, as loud as your refusal to shrink.

This book is not a manual. It will not tell you what to do or how to do it. That's not my role, and it's not your need. You don't need another checklist, you need to remember what you already know. My purpose here is not to hoard wisdom or posture as a guru. My purpose is to spread insight, to open doors, to leave a trail of keys.

Take what resonates, leave what doesn't. You are your own authority.

The chapters ahead are not "steps." They are keys. Each one unlocks something you already carry inside. Some will confront you. Some will comfort you. All of them are meant to remind you that your becoming is already happening. This book just puts language to what your spirit already whispers.

Read it straight through or skip to the chapter you feel pulled to. Sit with the rites and practices. Let the affirmations brand themselves into your memory. Return to what stirs you. Ignore what doesn't.

This is not about becoming like me. It's about becoming more of you.

SACRED AF

"No more shrinking. No more hiding. I claim my place, my power, my path."

SACRED AF

Ritual Architecture

Each Key is a rite of remembrance—an initiation into deeper self-mastery. Together they form a living architecture for becoming: nine structures of thought, discipline, and devotion that rebuild the Self from the inside out. You can follow them in sequence or move intuitively; either way, the path will meet you where you are and demand that you rise. Once you begin this work, you can't return to who you were before it.

MENTALISM 7
    The mind as sacred technology; every creation begins here.

EMBODIMENT 17
    Returning to the body: the first altar of truth and presence.

MANIFESTATION 25
    Stop creating on autopilot. Align word, thought, and ritual.

BOUNDARIES 33
    Every "no" builds the architecture of freedom.

TRANSFORMATION 43
    Die to performance so the real self can live unedited.

SELF-LOVE 53
    Love is not optional. It's the fuel and foundation of sovereignty.

CONSERVATION 61

 The mystic's path: silence, synchronicity, remembrance.

SOVEREIGNTY 71

 Choosing alignment over approval and authority over permission.

ENERGY CLEARING 83

 Clear what clouds your field; return to resonance.

THE FINAL RITE OF BECOMING 93

You seal the nine keys into your body, your breath, and your word.

INTRODUCTION

This is not a book of instructions. This is an initiation.

You will not find "five steps to self-love" or "ten hacks for manifestation" in these pages. What you will find is ignited fire. Stories, codes, and truths written from my own scars and revelations. This is not about convincing you. It's about reminding you all of what you already know.

This book exists to spark that knowing, not to replace it. To hand you keys, not cages. To inspire alignment, not obedience.

Sacred AF will not hold your hand. It will not flatter your excuses. It will not give you permission slips. It will provoke you. It will test you. It will dare you to walk out of the life you were scripted for and into the one you came here to author.

The voice here is direct because life is short. It's unapologetic because dilution is death. You don't have to agree with every word. In fact, I hope some pages piss you off because agitation is often the doorway to awakening.

Each key in this book includes Sacred Practices and Rites, simple ways to move the work from the page into your body. Some are reflective, others ritual, all are invitations to embody what you've read. To deepen the experience, select chapters include companion soundscapes. Scan the QR code at the chapter's beginning to listen as you read, allowing the frequency to tune you into the lesson's vibration.

Read this book however you need to. Some keys may hit now, other years later. But know this: you are not being told what to do. You are being invited to remember who you are.

This is not self-help. This is sovereignty.

SACRED AF

SACRED AF: SOUND ESCAPES VOL. I- RITUAL GRADE EDITION

This is the ritual layer of Sacred AF, the sound beneath the words.

Each track in Sound Escapes Vol. I was composed to mirror a key within this book, weaving frequency, rhythm, and breath into your reading.

Scan the QR code below to experience a sample playlist of the Ritual Grade Edition or visit oraclekeys.com to access the full frequency download.

Listen while you read, move or rest. Let the vibration do what language can't.

SACRED AF

SACRED AF

CHAPTER ONE

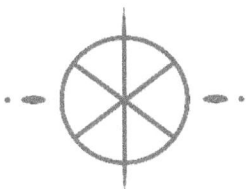

MENTALISM

*My mind is the first altar. Every thought is a blade, every image a spell.
The law is simple: when I think it, I build it.
Either I guard my mind or be ruled by another's design.*

Listen: Sacred AF- Mentalism Sound Escape (Ritual Grade Edition)

SACRED AF

You've heard the saying: *"You are what you eat."* But the truth is deeper: ***you are what you think.*** What you eat feeds your body, but what you think feeds your reality.

Mentalism is the First Key because *the Mind is ALL.*

Every prison, every freedom, every story you've ever lived started as a thought. You don't just think inside the universe, you are co-creating it with every thought you allow to take root. And yet, most of us live on autopilot.

We inherit beliefs, cultural programming, as well as the principles of parents, teachers, and lovers and they become the script we mistake for life. The truth is: every reality you've ever experienced was first a thought you agreed to.

Thoughts are not harmless. They are blueprints.

Mentalism begins with thought, but authorship gives thought direction. To think is to generate; to author is to design. You are not just the observer of your mind but the narrator of it. You are shaping the frequency that form will later obey.

When you don't claim authorship, your mind will keep building homes out of lies and illusions. Some of us live in shacks of scarcity, others in houses of people-pleasing, and some have built full mansions: lavish, impressive, but hollow.

The size of the structure doesn't matter if it was built on falsehoods. A mansion of illusions is still a prison.

This is why tearing down those structures feels so heavy. The bigger the dwelling, the harder it is to admit it was never real. You've decorated it with jobs, cars, titles, money; status symbols that look solid but crumble when truth knocks at the door.

If the foundation was a lie, then the **collapse is liberation.**

Collapse is terrifying, but it's the doorway. If you sit inside the structures you've built, while living in the truth of your becoming, you'll feel the walls closing in. That's resistance telling you: this version of you doesn't belong here anymore. What's more terrifying than existing instead of living? As the popular proverb says, 'Life is for the living.' But living and dying walk hand in hand. Collapse is the death required for your next life to begin.

This chapter isn't about "thinking positive." That's spiritual bypass, not mastery.

Thinking positive without discipline is not mastery but bypass. Bypass is denial of spiritual law, an attempt to sidestep its demands. Mastery is different. Mastery is alignment as the deliberate practice of working with law, not pretending it doesn't exist.

The trap of "just think positive" also creates the trap of emotional attachment. When you cling to an outcome with desperation, you swing with the pendulum of Hermetic law. High on hope one moment, crashing into despair the next.

Attachment turns your thoughts into chains instead of keys. True mental mastery isn't about forcing your mind to stay fixed on an outcome. It's about holding steady when the swing comes. You have to see both ends of the spectrum without letting either own you.

This initiation is about exposing the lies your mind has been looping, breaking their spell, and writing new ones that align with your highest becoming. Because the first spell is always a thought.

Here is where expectation comes in.

Expectation is the invisible contract your mind signed. What you believe will happen, happens. This is so, because energy bends towards expectation like a magnet.

This is why affirmations alone don't work. You can chant *"I am loved"* all day, but if your expectation is *"I'll be abandoned,"* guess which thought has the power? The one backed by belief. The one your mind already signed.

Expectations shape your reality before you even take a step. You've felt it when you walk into a room already expecting rejection, you find the cold shoulder. When you expect failure, you sabotage yourself before the first move. When you expect nothing, life provides nothing.

Most of us don't realize that expectations are related to our programming. Social engineering installs them like software as quiet contracts written in a language we never consented to. Every expectation you carry, conscious or not, is a line written into your operating system.

Family scripts, cultural myths, religious dogma, media cues… they shape our choices the way code shapes a simulation. That's why so many of us move through life like NPCs, non-player characters in someone else's game. We are animated but not awake.

When you break false expectations, you're not just "thinking differently." You're debugging the system.

You're finding the malware of "not enough," "play small," "follow the rules," and deleting it. Every broken contract is a line of corrupted code erased. Every new truth is a fresh line written in the language of your becoming is essential on this path.

To rebel against false expectations is to stop living inside someone else's spell. To burn the quiet contracts, you never chose and write new ones that reflect your becoming.

To face your shadow is to face your expectations. It's uncomfortable to admit that part of you expect to fail, to be unloved, to be overlooked. But until you name it, you keep living it.

By dumping the baggage of false expectations, you make room to write new ones that actually reflect who you are becoming and not who you've been. It is at this point that intentionality comes into play.

Once you've cleared the viruses, you have to choose what program runs next.

Your mind is sacred tech, and if you don't write the code, someone else will.

Every yes and every no become an input. Every choice is a command. Intentionality is not about control, it's about authorship.
Intentionality is what separates the rebels who thrive from the rebels who burn out.

Intentionality is wielding mentalism on purpose. It's the difference between scattering energy in a thousand directions and shaping it with clarity. Every yes, every no, every decision is an invocation. Your mind speaks, and the universe bends to listen.

This is about spiritual precision. It is not about doing more but about choosing with awareness. Every decision you make is an offering, and the universe responds to the vibration of that offering.

It is easy to burn out when you say yes to everything. The sacred no and the aligned yes become your compass once intentional. You don't need to push life around. You only need to choose with awareness, and reality rearranges around your decision.

Expectation is debugging the old code. Intentionality is writing the new one.

You are not powerless. You are not random. **You are a chooser.** Every choice is an invocation. Every yes or no is a spell.

Your thought patterns bend reality like metal in fire. If you think it's hard, it will be. If you expect rejection, the cold shoulder will meet you. But if you choose with clarity, your mind will carve reality into new form.

You are not just living in the world. You are living in the world your mind builds.

Your mind is ancient sacred technology, and Source will always make you right. So, it is the time to shape time, energy, and outcomes not by force, but by clarity.

There is no escaping the mind, and you must be clear on what you want to co-create with Source.

This is probably the most terrifying part of becoming because you have to own that you, yourself, are the creator of both the highs and the lows in this life. Terror stems from responsibility but the relief from that terror can only come from dominion of self. Mentalism requires decisiveness, awareness, and accountability if you're ready to hop off autopilot.

It makes no sense to say out of your mouth you are the architect of your life but still think in terms of victimhood and helplessness. You can't have it both ways. Life reflects what you think because law doesn't play.

As above, so below. As within, so without. It doesn't miss, whether you are active or reactive in your thought process.

Whether you realize it or not, your reality bends itself to the room you create internally first. Each moment you decide if you want to live in calm or chaos. And make no mistake:

YOU, my love, are the creator of worlds and Source will always make you right.

What you eat feeds your body. What you think feeds your reality. And reality is hungry. What will you feed it?"

Sacred Practice: Thought Audit

Catch one thought today that drags you down. Don't excuse it, don't dress it up; grab it. Now speak out loud: *"Not my spell."* Replace it with a sharper one that matches the life you're actually building. Do this three times today, minimum.

Sacred Rite: The Thought Altar

Anchor:
Every story you live begins as a thought. This rite is about exposing the hidden scripts running in your mind, breaking their spell, and planting a new one. The mirror doesn't lie, it reflects exactly what your mind has been rehearsing.

The Rite:
- Find a mirror. Sit or stand in front of it. Look directly into your eyes.
- Speak one thought you've been rehearsing that keeps you small (*ex: "I always mess things up"*). Say it out loud. Watch your reflection as you hear the words land.
- Now, cross your arms in front of your chest. Break the spell with: *"This thought is not law."*
- Replace it: declare a new thought aligned with your becoming (*ex:*

"I am the architect of my life"). Repeat it three times, watching your reflection as you claim it.
- Seal it by touching your forehead and whispering: *"As within, so without. My mind creates my world."*

Integration:
Repeat this rite whenever you catch yourself spiraling in mental loops. The mind doesn't stop creating but you get to choose which thoughts become law.

Reflection Prompt: What thought did you break today? What new blueprint are you building instead?

Closing Affirmation (Seal)

"My mind is the architect. My thoughts are the spell. I claim authorship of my reality, and I choose with clarity, alignment, and power. The Mind is ALL, and I am its rebel creator."

Closing Key

"The mind is the first altar. Guard it, and the world will kneel to your blueprint."

SACRED AF

CHAPTER TWO

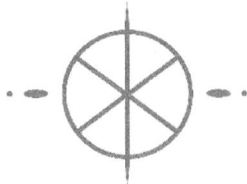

EMBODIMENT

Truth is nothing until I live it. My body is the archive. My walk is the proof. Embodiment is not theory — it is my word made flesh. Without it, I am fluent in nothing.

Listen: Sacred AF- Embodiment Sound Escape (Ritual Grade Edition)

SACRED AF

Knowledge without embodiment is just decoration. You can stack books, memorize verses, collect crystals and tarot decks but if you don't live it, it's costume jewelry. Pretty, but powerless.

For a long time, that was me. I had the altars, the palo santo, the oracle cards, and the tools. I read book after book, convinced I was growing because my shelves were full. But I wasn't living it. I was a pseudo-metaphysician: fluent in theory, starving in practice.

Embodiment is the revolution against theory.

It's the point where what you know either becomes who you are or proves it was just a hobby.

I had to learn this the hard way. At one point, I didn't even want to read anymore. Every book, every tool started to feel like a crutch. The more I read, the more I relied on something outside of myself to tell me the "right" way to become. But that only kept me stuck in the first stage: gathering information and looping on it endlessly.

Information without action was my excuse not to act.

I told myself I couldn't move forward without the right oil, the right herb, the exact ritual. If I didn't do it like the book prescribed, then it wouldn't work. But that's the trap.

Books are guidance, not gospel. They are mirrors, not masters. They are reference points for when are drawn to intrinsic knowing, not laws that dictate your path.

Once I stopped worshiping the words of others as "Lord and Law" of my becoming, I finally moved. I stepped into my own sacred ways. And that shift, from waiting for someone else's instructions to embodying my own truth is when embodiment actually began.

Everything shifted when I stopped treating spirituality like a pastime and started honoring it as a path. I changed my new year to the Spring Equinox instead of the Gregorian calendar. I studied my natal chart and numerology, not as curiosity but as mirrors to live by. I began aligning with the seasons and planetary rhythms, honoring cycles instead of resisting them.

I didn't just study the chart. I became the chart.

That shift wasn't aesthetic, it was quantum. Because the truth is, embodiment is what closes the gap between knowing and becoming.

What I need you to understand is spirituality isn't cosplay. It isn't a costume you put on to prove your "light" to others.

If you really are love, why do you need the performance?

Your spirituality is private, sacred, and should be protected. You are Spirit. It's who you are naked and stripped down; no stage lights, no audience, no mask.

Silence is protection.
Stillness is protection.
Being is protection.
Because silence, stillness and being are sacred acts.

Embodiment at its deepest is also love. Before my twin flame, I performed love. I rationalized it. I thought myself into and out of it because that's what I knew how to do. But with him, for the first time, I felt it. I embodied it. I became love. It wasn't effort. It wasn't performance. It was safe, because space was held for me to simply be.

That's what embodiment asks of you: to stop rushing from one thing to the next, to stop trying to force, push, or manipulate life into shape and just be. Pure existence, unbothered. That is love in its rawest form: not seeking, not proving, simply inhabiting what you already are.

Surround yourself with people who allow you to embody your source code. Hold space for yourself the same way. Give yourself full permission to sync with your essence not in theory, not in performance, but in lived presence.

I thought embodiment had to look like ceremony. Big altars. Elaborate rituals. Perfect tools. I imagined it as something grand, maybe even unattainable unless all the conditions lined up. But then one morning on a Virgo New Moon, it clicked.

I felt restless and scattered and tried to think my way out of it. When that didn't work, I sat still and realized I needed to be in my body. Virgo is an earth sign, and earth calls us back to grounding, to the material, to presence.

So, I broke my fast early with a cup of coffee, raw sugar and creamer swirling in. When I took that first sip, Self whispered, *"This self-care is true embodiment."*

It stopped me in my tracks. How could this cup of coffee be embodiment? This is too simple. It didn't happen later, when I felt more 'ready.' Not when the candles were lit or the crystals lined up just right. Embodiment was happening in real time; in a sip, in the warmth filling me, in the simple act of letting myself be here.

That was the shock. The realization that embodiment isn't always dramatic. It isn't always dressed in ritual clothing. Sometimes it's as ordinary as honoring your body with food after a fast or grounding your nervous system with warmth. It's not as grandiose as you thought, huh?

Because embodiment is not about how it looks. It's about whether you're *in it.* Whether you're present enough to catch that the sacred is already here, woven into the simplest choices.

We've come to an era where people talk "love and light" but there's no proof in their walk. They preach alignment but live in chaos. They speak abundance but embody lack.

The raw truth is to be spiritual does not mean to live poorly, in limitations, or in struggle. That's not holiness, that's ego disguised as humility.

If you embody Source, you embody limitlessness. You embody abundance. You embody power.

Embodiment is walking your truth until it imprints on your energy field so strongly that it emanates outward without you ever needing to announce it.

When you embody, you don't have to declare you're spiritual. You attract what you are.

But embodiment is not rigid. It is flow.

And when I speak of flow, I don't mean drifting aimlessly, surrendering to chaos, or letting life toss you around. That is not true flow.

Flow is adaptability. Flow is radical awareness.

When you are in flow, you recognize when synchronicities, downloads, and opportunities are staring you in the face. You have the courage to pivot, to shift, to follow the current that's alive.

To be married to how something should look, feel, or be is to cling to dead weight. There is no growth in that, only stagnation.

Flow is the art of syncing with what is alive and undeniable.

Nothing in this realm stays the same. Everything is cyclical and dynamic. Embodiment is choosing not to fight that truth but to move with it.

Stop fighting for the fantasy. Stop clinging to the corpse of an old story. Instead, bend reality to your will by living in ease and flow. Because embodiment and flow are not separate, they are one.

To embody is to live in flow, to let your knowing move through you so fully that life itself becomes your ritual. No masks, no performance, no resistance. Just Spirit, alive and unfiltered, walking the world as you.

Embodiment is flow. Flow is embodiment. And when you live in it, the world has no choice but to bend to what you are.

Sacred Practice: Silent Proof

Before you reach for tools, rituals, or performances… stop. Strip it down. Sit in silence for 5 minutes and let your energy speak without a costume. Ask yourself: *"If no one knew I was spiritual, would my life prove it?"*

Sacred Rite: The Silent Proof

Anchor:
Embodiment is not theory. It's not decoration. It's not performance. True embodiment is proven in silence, when there are no tools, no incense, no eyes watching. This rite strips you down to the essence of Spirit, reminding you that who you are in stillness is enough.

The Rite:
- Strip away all tools. No altar, no cards, no incense. Just you.
- Sit in silence for **11 minutes**. Breathe. Be. No performance, no display.
- Place your hand on your heart and whisper: *"I AM Spirit. I AM enough without adornment."*
- When you rise, notice how your energy speaks louder than any ritual you've ever performed.

Integration:
Do this rite often, especially when you feel the pull to prove your spirituality to others. This practice recalibrates you to simplicity: your being is the only altar you need.

Reflection Prompt:
What did silence reveal to you about your essence? How does your energy speak when there are no words, no costumes, no tools?

Closing Affirmation (Seal)
"I live rooted in my body. My presence is proof. I embody Source in every breath and every step."

Closing Key:
Embodiment is not theory–it is the truth made flesh.

CHAPTER THREE

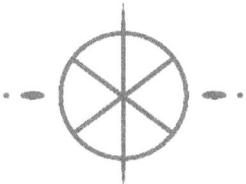

MANIFESTATION

*Creation is not wishful thinking. It is contract. It is law.
What I seed in energy, words, and action returns as my world.
Fantasy is cheap. Manifestation is precise.*

Listen: Sacred AF- Manifestation Sound Escape (Ritual Grade Edition)

SACRED AF

Manifestation is not separate from thought and embodiment, **it is their offspring.**

How do you know what you are creating in this realm?

Your life is the audit of your becoming.

Multiplication doesn't lie. You don't get what you want, you get what you are.

For years, I lived like I didn't deserve rest. I told myself I couldn't buy a bed until my business was profitable. I turned my bedroom into an office, slept on a futon, sometimes on a couch, believing that hustle earned worthiness.

One day, I decided enough. I deserved a space that reflected me, not just my grind. I tore up the carpet, laid down new floors, painted the walls, bought myself a bed and furniture that made me feel alive. I turned that one bedroom into a sanctuary.

That was November 2016. By April 2017, I was holding the keys to my first home. I was a homeowner of a three-bedroom, two-and-a-half-bath townhouse with a garage I had written about in my journal back in 2013. Line for line, it was the house I authored.

Manifestation didn't show up because I begged. It showed up because I aligned.

I honored the space I had, and the Universe mirrored it back with more. That's the law: **you don't multiply neglect into increase. You multiply honor into expansion.**

You can beg for more, but if you don't honor what you already hold, there is no room for multiplication. If you treat your current harvest with contempt, the field has no reason to multiply it.

Manifestation is not about craving more. It is about aligning with who you are becoming, honoring what you hold now, and opening room for creation to multiply.

Look around. That is your law in form.

Manifestation is the math of energy + action + alignment. You've been manifesting your whole life; every cycle, every pattern, every "coincidence" that kept showing up. You've manifested blessings. You've manifested disasters. The question isn't whether you manifest, it's whether you're doing it on autopilot or on purpose.

The world watered manifestation down into aesthetics, pretty pictures and empty slogans. Vision boards without vision. Wish lists without will.

Manifestation isn't about performance. It's about power.

It's not what you stage, it's what you live. Manifestation is not about begging the universe like it's Santa Claus. It's not about hoping something falls into your lap if you say it enough times.

At its core, manifestation is rebellion against unconscious living.

Manifestation is not cute. It's contractual.

Every phrase you speak "I always attract the wrong people," "money never sticks," "nothing ever works out for me" is a contract. The universe, neutral and obedient, delivers onto the contract you authored. Not because it's cruel. Not because it plays favorites. But because law doesn't fail.

Failure, heartbreak, disappointment as these too are manifestations. They are not punishments. They are initiations.

Your job isn't to control the *how*. Your job is to align with the *why* and the *what*, then stay available for the ways it can unfold.

Manifestation fails when it becomes emotional blackmail. You grip so tightly to what you want that you confuse obsession with alignment. But obsession is still attachment, and attachment bends you into desperation instead of flow.

Here's the code: manifestation isn't about begging or bargaining with the universe. It's not "if I want it badly enough, it has to come." That's invoking the pendulum swing; clinging to the swing toward desire and fearing the swing back into lack.

The law is more precise than that.

You want to manifest from clarity, not from clenching.

Expectation without attachment is where balance is achieved. It's declaring, "This is mine," and releasing the how. It's when you have faith in the soil after you plant the seed instead of digging it up to see if it's growing daily.

True power begins when you write the contracts that represent your truth and stop signing the contracts you didn't mean to draft.

That means restraint with your thoughts, audacity with your words, and follow-through with your actions. Energy bends toward clarity. The universe is like a mirror; it reflects what you *are*, not what you pretend to want.

Here's the code most people miss: **Be → Do → Have.**

But most people flip the formula. They chase the *Have*: the car, the money, the partner. They force the *Do*: hustling, striving, grasping. And they skip the *Be* altogether. That's why what they manifest never lasts. It slips through their fingers, because the foundation was never alive inside them.

You don't manifest from hustle. You manifest from being.

The universe doesn't respond to your hustle. It responds to your frequency. You manifest from who you *are* during your process, *not* from what you do.

- **Be** is your state, your belief, your vibration. It's who you are before the world responds.

- **Do** is the action that naturally flows from that state. Not forced but aligned.
- **Have** is the effect. The fruit that grows from the seed of your being and doing.

This is the law of cause and effect. Not metaphysical fluff but actual law. Every cause creates an effect. So, every single thought, word, ritual is a cause. The effect must follow. The universe doesn't care whether the cause was conscious or unconscious. It just multiplies the input.

This is why manifestation is less about "getting what you want" and more about *becoming who you must be* so what you want has no choice but to meet you.

Be → Do → Have in action looks like this:

Be first. Align your state. Embody the energy of the reality you desire.
Do next. Take actions that match that state. Small or large but aligned.
Have last. Watching the results materialize—not as miracles, but as math.

Being comes first: the discipline of choosing your state before you see evidence. Becoming the person who is already worthy, already abundant, already whole.

Doing flows next: action that matches your being. No more half-hearted "tries" that contradict your inner vibration. When you *become,* your doing sharpens into precision.

Having is the effect: what you embody and move in, the universe mirrors back. Cause → effect. No exceptions.

Every closed door, every failure, every moment of "this isn't working" was the universe cashing in on the contracts you wrote unconsciously. It was law doing what law does. It reflects back the evidence of the state of being and doing you were carrying at the time. That's why they stung: they reveal the code you were running. And every code can be rewritten.

Stop pretending you're powerless. Stop outsourcing your life to chance. Start writing contracts on purpose.

Manifestation is not magic dust. **It's rebellion against unconscious creation. It's authorship.** It's the audacity to stop living on autopilot and to write contracts with the universe you actually mean to sign.

Narration is manifestation in motion. Every story you tell about yourself becomes architecture for reality to build on. To narrate consciously is to script frequency into form; to choose words that align with the future you intend, not the past you survived. Authorship is the bridge: the act of naming your becoming until matter remembers.

This isn't about begging the universe. It's about being deliberate; matching your frequency to your intention so tightly that reality has no choice but to rearrange.

You don't manifest what you want. You manifest what you are.

So, the question becomes: who are you willing to *be*?

Sacred Practice: Break the Spell

Listen to the words you toss around casually. Every "I'm broke," "nobody stays," "just my luck" is a contract. The next time one slips out, stop and declare: *"Cancel. Rewrite."* Then replace it with a statement that bends toward your becoming. Speak it three times like law.

Sacred Rite: Sigil Creation

Anchor:
Every word you speak is a contract. Every thought is a spell. Sigils

distill your intention into a symbol that bypasses language and speaks directly to the subconscious. This rite transforms vague desire into deliberate creation.

The Rite:
- Write down one sentence that states your intention (ex: *"I live in peace and abundance"*).
- Cross out all repeating letters.
- With the remaining letters, design a simple symbol. Let it emerge more than you "plan" it.
- Charge it: trace it in the air, draw it on your skin, whisper it over water, or place it under your pillow.

Integration:
This is now a living contract. Return to it when you need to remember what you chose. Charge it again anytime it begins to fade from your energy field.

Reflection Prompt:
What did you notice in your body as you created your sigil? Did the symbol feel familiar, new, or both?

Closing Affirmation (Seal)

"I create on purpose. My energy, my words, my actions all speak the same truth: I am aligned with the life I came here to live."

Closing Key

Cause creates effect. Write the cause, and the effect has no choice.

SACRED AF

CHAPTER FOUR

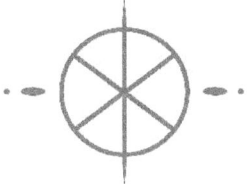

BOUNDARIES

My no is a holy spell. A line drawn in sovereignty is my map back to freedom. My boundaries are not walls — they are thresholds. Cross them at your own cost.

Listen: Sacred AF- Boundaries Sound Escape (Ritual Grade Edition)

SACRED AF

Boundaries are spiritual architecture.

Without them, your energy is a house with broken doors and shattered windows. Anyone can walk in, take what they want, and leave you depleted.

But here's the code: most of us were taught that boundaries are selfish, harsh, or unloving. So, we bleed ourselves dry trying to be agreeable, dependable, and "easy to love." That's not love. That's self-erasure.

We've been trained to look out the window more than look in the mirror. To concern ourselves with everything outside of us, only to end up further from our path. Everyone thinks martyrdom makes you good, but all it makes is a false identity: playing nice to be called nice.

The pull to be "nice" is one of the most seductive traps. Good people want to be seen as good. But **niceness isn't goodness. Niceness is performance.**

We learn early that if we play nice, we'll be named nice. We'll be praised as the good one, the easy one, the agreeable one. But niceness has a cost: it asks you to abandon yourself for approval.

Boundaries will not let you pay that price. Boundaries are not about being palatable. It's about being true.

When you contort yourself into someone else's idea of "good," you trade authenticity for applause. That's not love. That's theater.

A boundary enforced from truth may look like cruelty to those still living in performance. It means you stop auditioning for the role of "nice", be willing to be misnamed and take your rightful place as sovereign.

You are not here to be agreeable and perform. You are

here to be whole.

Majority of people don't know who they are, so why should their opinion rule yours? Not wanting to be misunderstood is the fastest path to sabotaging your own sovereignty. You'll build boundaries you never enforce.

Boundaries are not about pushing people away. They protect the sanctity of your inner temple, so that when you open the door, it is by choice not obligation. They are not cages. They are sacred architecture. They honor your energy as holy ground because you are holy.

Still, most take boundaries as rejection. They hear your no as wound, your distance as judgment, your silence as punishment. They were never taught sovereignty, so they are offended at yours.

A boundary is not punishment because punishment is control. **A boundary is clarity. It is redirection toward your freedom, your wholeness, your true relationships.**

It takes time for the spiritually gifted to understand detachment: that relationship titles do not guarantee safe spaces. You'll hold space for manipulators, excuse their behavior, hoping to witness their becoming. You'll do it until you're exhausted then you'll see clearly. They are who they are. That has nothing to do with you. Make peace with that.

Every soul came here with an assignment. Some came to party. Some came to anchor divine frequency. It's on you to accept people as they are, not as you want them to be. **Stand ten toes down. Require respect for your boundaries. Anyone who resents that is just a line-crosser, unwilling to grow.**

You may be tempted to shrink to be relatable, to prove you're still the same. But for what? For company that can't hold your real self. There is no shame in growth. The shame is letting others guilt you for becoming more.

When I walk out of a room where the frequency is heavy, I'm not declaring myself better than anyone. I'm declaring myself unwilling to suffocate. My leaving is not about them; it's about protecting the field I live in.

Enforcing boundaries may look like arrogance to those who've never chosen themselves. Arrogance is sovereignty misnamed by the insecure. It's the audacity to be bigger than the box you were handed.

Arrogance is not puffed-up pride, it is resonance.

It's what happens when certainty vibrates louder than approval. The world taught you to mute that frequency because self-assured people are hard to manipulate. But arrogance is not a flaw; it's the energetic signature of alignment. It is the sound of a soul that refuses to apologize for accuracy.

When you are arrogant in your truth, you're not performing superiority, you're embodying precision. You've calibrated your frequency so tightly to your purpose that doubt can't find a foothold.

The meek view arrogance negatively because they mistake clarity for threat. Real arrogance, arrogance that is sacred, is the clean burn of knowing you are *custom built* in your divinity. Not bigger, not smaller, simply whole.

Be arrogant enough to believe in your own calibration. Be arrogant enough to rest when the world demands hustle. Be arrogant enough to walk away without closing the door softly behind you.

Arrogance is not ego. It is energetic dominion. It's the posture of someone who stopped auditioning for access to their own throne.

I was branded arrogant long before I claimed it. I wear it on my skin. Not because I think I am better than you, but because I refuse to be worse than myself.

If my presence disturbs your dysfunction, then my absence is compassion.

On the flip side, silence can be mistaken for passive aggression. The key is clarity, not resentment. The line between confrontation and conservation isn't tone—it's intention.

- **Confrontation from sovereignty**: calling a thing what it is, without venom.
- **Conservation from sovereignty**: leaving the table, not to punish, but to preserve your frequency.

Both are acts of freedom. Neither requires apology.

The hardest boundaries are with family, because family feels entitled to your yes. When you say no, they call it immaturity, mistake it for confusion, press harder.

The Sacred No needs no diploma. It doesn't graduate into yes. It is complete by itself. "No means no" until the no is directed at them. Then suddenly, no is negotiable.

That assumption, that no must come from ignorance is projection. Often, it's the opposite. No is born from clarity. **No is the recognition that what is offered doesn't honor your becoming.**

Saying no to family will cost you the image of being "the good one." Being good in their script means being compliant. Compliance is not goodness. It is self-destruction.

The code is this: My no is wisdom. My no is enough. My no requires

no permission. Respect it or not, it still stands.

The moment you start explaining a boundary, you're leaking. Explanation is buying approval you don't need. Misunderstanding is inevitable when people don't even understand themselves. Every extra sentence is a receipt you didn't need to print.

Explaining your stance is another costume in the theater of approval. It's saying: "Don't misunderstand me, please still like me." But sovereignty doesn't audition. It writes the script and inspires the production.

A true boundary doesn't plead. It doesn't justify. It declares.

Let them call it harsh. Let them call it selfish. The point of a boundary is not to be understood. The point is to be free.

Most hear "boundaries" and think of defense: saying no, blocking energy, guarding peace. That's valid. But that's only half.
The other half is inward. Boundaries with yourself. This is where the **Law of Discipline** enters.

Feelings rise and fall like tides in the ocean. Intuition does not. Intuition is steady, but without discipline, feelings sabotage what you already know. *"I don't feel like it"* becomes the silent killer of purpose.

Discipline is the boundary that keeps you from crossing your own line. It isn't punishment, it's protection. Think of it as gestation: a seed in soil. The soil holds it in place until it's strong enough to sprout. Discipline is that soil. It holds your potential long enough to root.

Commitment is discipline stretched over time.

You set the boundary, then you honor it again and again. That honoring builds the bridge between where you are and where you're headed.

Without it, you restart forever. With it, depth forms and options multiply.

The "Sacred No" turns inward as discipline not as performance, but as essence. Discipline is not what you do but who you are when you move as law itself, steady and unshakable. To refuse yourself is to reveal yourself: each No to distraction is a Yes to sovereignty.

The alchemy of boundaries is that they don't shrink you, they expand you.

- External boundaries: *I decide what gets in.*
- Internal boundaries: *I decide what won't leak out before it's ready.*

Together, they incubate your evolution.

Boundaries are not walls. They are wombs. They don't just protect your freedom, they gestate it.

Sacred Practice: The Sacred No

Today, say no once where you'd normally cave. Don't over-explain. Don't apologize. Just *no*. Then notice what happens in your body. That tightening in your chest? That's freedom waking up.

Sacred Rite: The Sacred No

Anchor:
Every "no" is not rejection, it is redirection. Saying no is not about shutting the world out, it is about protecting the sanctity of your temple. Most of us were conditioned to believe that boundaries make us cold, difficult, or unloving. The Sacred No dismantles that lie. This rite rewires

your body and spirit to experience "no" as protection, reclamation, and power.

The Rite:
Take a sheet of paper. Write down one thing in your life where you keep saying "yes" when your soul is begging you to say "no." Name it honestly.

Across the words, in bold letters, write **NO.** Make it large, undeniable, a scar that cannot be erased.

Now stand tall. Say the "no" out loud three different ways: firm, playful, and unapologetic. Feel the shift in your body as you release the performance and step into truth.

As the final seal, place your hand over your heart and whisper: *"This no protects me. This no honors me. This no frees me."*

Integration:
Repeat this rite anytime you feel guilt rising when you say no. Over time, your body will remember that "no" is not selfish — it is sacred architecture.

Reflection Prompt:
What fear comes up for you when you say no? How can you reframe that fear as freedom?

Closing Affirmation (Seal)

"My no is sacred. It guards the threshold of my temple and protects the holy ground of my becoming."

Closing Key

A boundary is not a wall-it is the threshold where only truth is allowed to live.

SACRED AF

CHAPTER FIVE

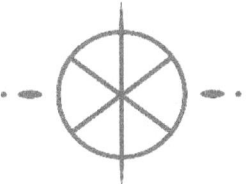

TRANSFORMATION

My collapse is not the end — it is my portal.
Fire does not return me the same. My ashes lay fertile ground, and rebirth is my law.
Transformation is the unmaking that makes me more.

Listen: Sacred AF- Transformation Sound Escape (Ritual Grade Edition)

SACRED AF

Transformation is never polite. It does not knock on the door of your life and ask permission to enter. It kicks it open.

It demands you release what no longer carries truth, even if that "truth" was all you knew.

We are taught that transformation is clean, shiny, effortless, glow-up energy. New hair, new job, new vibe. But real transformation doesn't start with what you add. It starts with what you lose. It is the undoing of everything false that once held you together.

The first language of transformation is grief. **Something must die for you to live differently.** An identity. A relationship. A dream. A version of you that cannot make the next chapter. And when that death comes, it tears through you. It rearranges the furniture of your soul whether you gave permission or not.

Most people avoid transformation because it costs too much: comfort, identity, relationships, certainty. But to rebel against stagnation is to say:

I will not stay dead while I am alive.

This path asks you to face destruction without flinching, to let go of the old skins that suffocate you, to stand in the fire long enough for what's false to burn off. Only then does the truth emerge as lighter, sharper, unstoppable.

When my son Alchemy came into my life, I knew his name before I knew his face. I knew he was here to transform me. And he did.

Alchemy's time earthside was brief, but his impact eternal. When he passed, people expected me to fall apart in a way they could understand loud, visible, endless breakdowns. Because that kind of grief makes others comfortable.

But I didn't fall apart the way they expected. Not because I didn't feel it, but because transformation asked something different of me. The spiritual part of me understood that death is a natural and guaranteed part of life. What I never fathomed was ever telling my 16-day-old son that it's okay if he decided not to stay, mommy and daddy will be okay. I knew the choice was ultimately up to him, and I trusted this precious soul to do what was part of our contract.

The battle of trying to determine if I had processed the trauma or if the trauma of loss was still alive in me was torture. Each birthday and milestone, I grieved one son and celebrated his twin, Khemistry. I held both devastation and wonder, both endings and beginnings, heartache and healing in the same heartbeat.

Most people and most relationships do not survive the death of a child. It is a hurt that is soul deep. One that is never "recovered" from.

What you do is you live because you must. Crumbling was not an option. This loss was the catalyst for me to be more than I ever dreamed of in mind, body, and spirit.

Alchemy's life and death called me to redefine success. What I thought it was and what I chased turned to ash.

Success was not the grind, not the appearance, not the applause. Success became presence, integrity, and wholeness.

His fire authored me into something new.

People expect transformation to look like crisis, but sometimes it looks like standing in the ashes and refusing to let the fire consume you. Because ashes are not waste. **They are receipts**… evidence that what tried to contain you could not.

All because I carried my grief differently, people assumed I didn't need support. They mistook survival for strength, composure for numbness.

Transformation doesn't just strip the stage. It reveals who can stand with you in the fire and who only walks with you when the road is smooth.

Alchemy lived up to his name. He made me a living paradox: broken and whole, grieving and grateful, spirit and human. His life and death initiated me into transformation in a way no book or teaching ever could.

Beyond grief, transformation is an oxymoron. It is an impossible marriage of grief and joy, endings and beginnings, devastation and wonder.

Transformation does not ask you to choose. It demands you carry both.

It will feel like contradiction, but it is wholeness. I didn't become whole by choosing sides. I became whole by refusing to split myself, by fusing contradictions into truth.

This is the ancestral weight of transformation: it is rebellion. It is the vow:

"I refuse to inherit the silence. I refuse to rehearse the same self-betrayal. I refuse to repeat the lineage of abandonment."

Transformation breaks false altars. It smashes the rules that tell you to shrink, to hush, to play dead. Those rules do not survive fire.

What no one ever tells you is transformation feels like ruin before it feels like resurrection. You will wonder if you've lost your mind. You will think you've gone too far. But the burning is not punishment, it is purification.

Transformation is polarity in motion. Grief does not erase joy. Death does not erase life. Endings do not erase beginnings. They live together, side by side, remaking you as they collide.

Transformation dismantles the teachings you inherited about who you were supposed to be. The doctrines about strength, grief, survival, the ones you were handed like law are the first to collapse. Transformation begins when you recognize those beliefs cannot carry you through fire.

But it doesn't only burn your surface. It burns your inheritance.

Inheritance is more than property or heirlooms. It is contracts, silences, false altars you bowed to because you were told survival depended on it. Fire does not respect those contracts.

Transformation forces you to decide: will you repeat the lineage of self-abandonment, or will you end it here?

Does this stop with you? Will you be the one to break the generational curse?

Every time you step into fire and refuse to shrink, you're not only transforming yourself. You are liberating your lineage. The gift of transformation is not that you will never burn again. It is that you stop fearing flames.

You stop mistaking hardship for failure. You stop fearing endings because you know they are also beginnings.

I used to drag ghosts into my future. I kept chasing old versions of people, trying to force them into my becoming. But chasing ghosts only left me haunted.

Everyone isn't meant to survive the next version of you. Everyone isn't meant to walk through your fire. Leaving them behind isn't cruelty. It's precision.

I wish them well, but I refuse to be dragged down by the choices they make for themselves. Their path is theirs. My path is mine. That's the line. That's the transformation.

Real transformation is not glow-up. It is unmaking. It doesn't make life easier. It makes you unshakable. Because once you have walked through fire and risen from ashes, what can threaten you?

The question is not: *Will you survive?* The question is: *Will you allow it to make you new?*

The law of cycles says change is constant. Transformation is destruction and creation, collapse and rebirth. Sometimes you must burn down to make space for new foundation.

But destruction is not the whole story.

Transformation is divine tailoring.

The fire cuts away what no longer fits and stitches you into who you were always becoming. Nothing stays the same, and neither should you. Transformation is an everlasting process of death and rebirth. Its gift is choice. You are not stuck in any situation in life, as you can always choose again.

Transformation doesn't end at the burn. It evolves into the blend. You are alchemizing chaos into harmony, showing how it is possible to integrate consciously after collapse.

It is easy to think you must throw it all away, but that signals you are not worthy of being kept. Transformation does not demand your erasure. It demands your fusion. You transmute what serves your highest becoming and release the rest.

Transformation is balance as alchemy, not balance as stillness. It is the fusion of shadows and light into something that "should not exist" but does, because you do.

This is the code: to hold extremes, to stay present, to fuse contradictions into coherence. Transformation is not about what people think of you in the fire. It is about who you become because of it.

Transformation is not a one-time event.

It is a lifelong agreement with fire. Every time life asks you to burn, you rise again as something truer.

That is the contract. That is the alchemy.

Sacred Practice: The Ash Test

Look at one part of your life that's dying: a habit, a role, a relationship. Ask: *"If this burned to the ground, what would rise in its place?"* Sit with the answer. That's the you waiting on the other side of fire.

Sacred Rite: Burn & Birth

Anchor:
Transformation requires death. To rise, something false must fall away. This rite is both funeral and birth, asking you to bury what no longer serves and declare the life beyond it.

The Rite:
- Write down one belief, habit, or role you're ready to release. Name it with honesty.

- Burn the paper in a fireproof dish (or tear it into pieces if fire isn't possible).
- Immediately after, write one sentence beginning with: *"I rise as…"*
- Speak it aloud as your rebirth declaration.

Integration:
The ashes are not just endings. They are soil for your becoming. Repeat as often as you need. Every rebirth is a gateway.

Reflection Prompt:
What did you bury? What new Self rose in its place?

Closing Affirmation (Seal)

"I surrender to the fire. I release what no longer lives in me and rise in truth."
Closing Key

Transformation is the fire that rewrites your code into something unbreakable.

SACRED AF

CHAPTER SIX

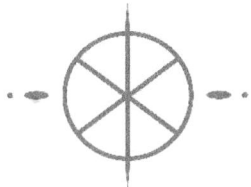

SELF-LOVE

My self-love is not comfort- it is command.
It is refusing to abandon myself for applause.
My greatest rebellion is choosing me, without apology.

Listen: Sacred AF- Self-Love Sound Escape (Ritual Grade Edition)

SACRED AF

The Self you meet after fire is not the one you left behind. That version burned in Transformation. What rises from the ashes is raw, unrecognizable, and often unwelcome to those who were comfortable with your old self. This is where Self-Love begins: **in the fierce embrace of the Self, you are becoming.**

You may find that this new Self unsettles people. They may accuse you of changing too much, of being hard to reach, of no longer being "the same." But the truth is, you *aren't* the same. Transformation did its work, and to betray this Self just to stay palatable would be to burn yourself all over again.

This Self must be loved and accepted more fiercely than ever.

Especially in the face of rejection. Especially in the face of pushbacks. It's because without that devotion to your essence, you risk slipping back into self-abandonment and that is death by another name.

In order to confront the lies you tell yourself, you cannot forgo self-love. Self-love will test you in ways unimaginable. It's a necessity for sovereignty because it allows you to see yourself in both your glory and your flaws and embrace your wholeness.

The world sells self-love as comfort and bliss: bubble baths, vacations, and the "soft life." What it fails to reveal is that real self-love is confrontation. It's drawing a line against every pattern of self-abandonment you've rehearsed. It's refusing to starve yourself of rest, joy, nourishment, and boundaries.

Self-love is not always soft.
Sometimes it is brutal honesty.
Sometimes it is discipline.
Sometimes it is walking away from the people or places that profit from your neglect.

The softness of faux self-love is momentary. True self-love sustains because it is built within, not borrowed from outside.

Day in and day out, you give your energy to the world. You allow everyone to feed off your power, only to end each day depleted. Self-love is being real about where your energy is going and whether there's a return on your investment.

The Law of Diminishing Returns makes it plain: keep pouring into something without balance, and the benefit decreases until it backfires. Burnout is the proof.

Relationships mirror the same law. You over give without return, and the result is depletion.

Self-love is discernment: knowing when what you've given is enough.

I learned this in a moment that never left me. The first time I told my twin flame I loved him, I didn't require him to say it back. I wasn't bargaining with love, hoping for a return. I was overflowing. I had love to give, and he was worthy to receive it. What he did with it was irrelevant, because my love was for me first. **That is the difference between depletion and abundance.**

When you give from lack, what you're essentially doing is bargaining with your energy. You're saying, "If I give you this, please return it back to me when I don't have it for myself." **This is debt, not love.** Giving from overflow is sovereignty. It's a gift, not a gamble, or a hustle. When you pour without overflow, you're bleeding out and misnaming it generosity.

You have to learn to become your own well. You have to re-parent yourself. Giving to your body, mind, and spirit what you may never have been taught to prioritize is how you grow beyond the neglect, pain, blame and shame.

What this looks like is giving yourself nurturing as well as boundaries you needed as a child but didn't necessarily receive. You are the mother and the father, the authority and the care now. Feeding yourself rest when you want to grind, giving yourself discipline when you want to avoid, and compassion when you want to breakdown is non-negotiable now.

Self-love is not coddling. It is governance. It is rebellion. It is the refusal: *I will not abandon myself the way the world has abandoned me.*

Self-love is loyalty to your essence, not allegiance to your mask. The mask demands allegiance because it is fragile. It has to be fed with performance, validation, and applause. Essence only asks for loyalty, because it is eternal.

But what if your essence really is put together? What if discipline, clarity, and sovereignty are not your costume but your core? Should you manufacture weakness just to earn grace from people who only recognize need when it looks like collapse?

The answer is no. You do not betray your essence to earn scraps of pity.

The world has been trained to respond to dysfunction, not sovereignty. People rush to the ones who are visibly crumbling, because their need is obvious, and helping them affirms the savior script. But when you stand sovereign; when you embody "togetherness" as truth, you are often overlooked, neglected, even punished. Support is withheld, not because you don't need it, but because your strength exposes their lack.

This is the trap: confusing "masking strength" with being strong. They are not the same.

- Masking strength is allegiance to the image: never let them see

you sweat.
- Being strong is loyalty to essence: I am whole, even when the room pretends not to see me.

Do not dim your wholeness to gain grace. Do not invent cracks just to be deemed worthy of care. If your sovereignty makes others blind to your humanity, that blindness is theirs to heal, not yours to fix.

Martyrs will parade their sacrifice, giving until depletion because they need the performance of need to secure their identity. You don't have to play that game. Your wholeness is not a mask. It is your inheritance.

Self-love is the refusal to trade your essence for their comfort.

Every act of radical care becomes a protest. Every "I am enough" that you act on becomes law.

Every time you choose to nourish yourself before pouring into others, you are rewriting the contracts of your lineage. You are declaring: *"I am worth protecting. I am worth feeding. I am worth the love I kept begging for outside of myself."*

The fastest way to abandon yourself is to believe your worth is proven by how much you are available to others. That is performance, not love. There is a double standard here. Others are allowed to excuse their absence but demand your constant presence. If you play along, resentment festers until avoidance becomes your only escape.

Self-love interrupts the contract. It declares: *My worth is not measured by exhaustion. My value is not tied to performance. My availability is not entitlement.*

This is the hardest kind of love because it asks you to face the mirror every day and decide that you are enough and then to act like it. Not just in words. In rituals. In choices. In how you treat yourself when no one is watching.

Self-love is not indulgence.
Self-love is alignment with truth.
Self-love is refusal to perform, to explain, or to be drained.
Self-love is authorship turned inward.

Do not carry what does not belong to you, even when the cost is the image of you as the pentacle of "goodness".

The rebellion here is radical: you stop waiting for someone else to save you, soothe you, or see you.

You become the love you've been waiting for.

Sacred Practice: Radical Self-Care Move

Choose one act of care you've been denying yourself (rest, food, joy, truth). Do it today, not tomorrow. Before you begin, say: *"This is law. This is love."* Don't negotiate. Don't guilt-trip yourself. Just do it.

Sacred Rite: Radical Care Act

Anchor:
Self-love is not indulgence. It is responsibility. This rite makes care non-negotiable by treating it as sacred action.

The Rite:
- Choose one act of care you've been denying yourself (sleep, food, joy, pleasure).
- Schedule it today. Not tomorrow. Today.

- Before you begin, place your hand over your heart and say: *"This is love in action. I am worth the responsibility of care."*
- Do it without guilt. Without apology.

Integration:
The more often you repeat this rite, the more your nervous system learns that care is not optional. It is your foundation.

Reflection Prompt:
How did it feel to give yourself what you've been withholding?

Closing Affirmation (Seal)

"I choose myself without apology. My care is my revolution.

Closing Key:

"The greatest rebellion is never leaving yourself behind."

CHAPTER SEVEN

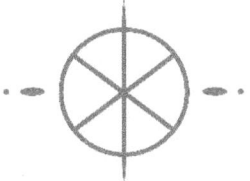

CONSERVATION

My power leaks where my words run wild.
My silence is not absence- it's concentrated presence.
When I conserve my energy, I rule my existence.

Listen: Sacred AF- Conservation Sound Escape (Ritual Grade Edition)

SACRED AF

Conservation is rebellion against consumption. We live in a world addicted to taking; to scrolling, to speaking, to proving, to buying. We're taught our worth is measured in output: **how much you produce, how much attention you can hold, how much of yourself you're willing to bleed for the crowd.**

But here's the code: *the world will never tell you to stop.* It will take and take until you are nothing but a carcass of "good intentions" and "endless giving."

Conservation says: Not today. Not ever again.

This key isn't glamorous. It's not loud. It's not marketable. It's silence when everyone wants noise. It's retreat when the world wants performance. **It's saying no without an apology attached.**

Conservation is about recognizing that your energy is **holy ground**. Every word, every thought, every offering is currency. *You don't hand it out like free samples.* You choose where it goes, and you cut the pipelines that leak your life force into people, systems, or addictions that don't honor it.

We've been programmed to confuse consumption with connection. We measure ourselves by likes, applause, and the echo chamber of "being seen." **But being seen isn't the same as being felt. Being heard isn't the same as being known.** Consumption is never satisfied.

This is why Conservation is a spiritual practice. It asks you to live on the edge of discomfort. To step back, to go silent, to withdraw your endless commentary and realize that *the only voice that actually matters is the one inside.*

No one is coming to save you, and you can't save anybody. You can only save yourself.

Stop trying to be the savior for everyone else. Stop trying to earn worthiness by bleeding out. You don't owe the world your burnout. You owe yourself, your becoming.

We like to think we all live in the same world. Same sun, same sky, same streets. But the truth is, we don't. We live in dimensions built by our perception, curated by our programming, and confirmed by what we choose to ingest.

It's no different from the feeds we scroll every day. Algorithms are mirrors of Mentalism. They don't show you "the world as it is." **They show you the world you've agreed to**. They amplify what you already believe, push you deeper into that reality, and mute out what doesn't align. Your "truth" is coded and confirmed by repetition. And the more you consume, the more you reinforce it.

This is why two people can live under the same roof and inhabit completely different worlds. One sees chaos everywhere, proof that humanity is doomed. The other sees opportunity, synchronicity, miracles hiding in plain sight. Who's right? Both of them. Because both are living in the dimension their mind has built.

This is the danger of unconscious conservation. You can live your entire life inside a carefully programmed bubble. It is fed to you by culture, by media, by generational myths. You become like a character in someone else's simulation, scripted by someone else's code.

When you wake up to this, you reclaim choice. You begin to conserve your energy differently. You stop pouring your attention into distractions that drain and distort you, and you start curating what nourishes your dimension. You become ruthless about what you let in. Regardless of whether it's conversations, content, environments, even your own thought loops because you realize every single thing you ingest is programming your dimension.

Reality is elastic. It bends not to "what's true" universally, but to what's true to you.

And when you grasp this, you stop arguing about other people's realities. You stop needing everyone to see what you see. You stop wasting your energy trying to prove your dimension is the "right" one. Instead, you put that energy into refining the one you're actually living in.

Conservation, then, becomes sovereignty-in-practice. It's not just about protecting your energy. It's always about protecting your dimension. **Every word, every image, every song, every thought is an ingredient. And the dimension you walk through is the recipe.**

So, ask yourself: are you living in a feed that frees you, or a feed that cages you?

Are you conserving energy in alignment with the dimension you're becoming, or hemorrhaging energy to keep alive a world you don't even believe in anymore?

Because you don't just live in the world. You live in the world your mind builds, and Conservation is how you choose which one it will be.

Conservation is the art of holding. *Holding your tongue. Holding your energy. Holding your mystery.* Because what is conserved builds pressure, and what builds pressure becomes power.

When you conserve, you stop scattering your light like cheap confetti. You hold it close, and when you finally release it, **it lands with weight. It lands with truth. It lands with force.**

Conservation is sacred minimalism. Not in the sense of aesthetic, but in the soul sense. It strips away the noise so only what matters remains. If you master this key, you won't need to announce yourself.

Your silence will say more than your speeches. Your restraint will carry more power than your performances. And when you do speak, the world will stop and listen.

Start to think about your energy like an economy. Economics is the study of choices. It's what we spend, what we save and what we harvest. Your energy should be treated in the same way.

Every yes is an investment. Every no is a refusal to fund that which drains you. Every vow of silence is interest earned from your power.

It's at this point a deeper understanding emerges. I had to understand that when I waste words, I am leaking currency. When I overgive I subsidize someone else's chaos. When I explain myself for approval, I take out a loan I can never repay.

Spending looks like speech, habits, attention and people. Savings look like silence, restraint and solitude. Return on investment or your harvest looks like rest, ritual and aligned action.

I had to get real with myself and accept that my energy is not infinite although it is sovereign. I decided what receives it. I decide what cuts it off. I decided how to invest and store energy back into myself.

This is what an energy economy looks like: deliberate, disciplined and divine. Don't waste it. Don't trade it cheap. Conserve it so you can reign.

Overgiving is one of the deepest leaks. Not because people demand it, but because programming whispers that you'll never be enough unless you do more, give more, prove more.

Guilt disguises itself as generosity.

But generosity without Conservation is not love, it is leakage. It is a quiet attempt to purchase worthiness with exhaustion.

True generosity flows from overflow. But when you give from lack, you are bargaining. That is not *love*. That is **debt**. Conservation interrupts the cycle by saying: *enough is enough*. My value is not proven by depletion.

Anything done in avoidance is also a leak. It doesn't matter if it looks harmless. Scrolling, noise, busyness, distractions; they are all modern opiates. They mask themselves as comfort, but they are really avoiding. And every moment you leak into avoidance is a moment stolen from your becoming.

Conservation demands that you stop medicating your restlessness and instead face it. Because once you face yourself, you reclaim the energy you used to waste on avoidance.

I remember this particular day; I sat at my desk sick. My body was begging for rest, but my programming was louder: *stay, push, prove you're dependable, keep your place safe*. That's what I was taught, that sickness is weakness, and weakness is a liability.

But as I sat there, drained and dizzy, I realized: this is the trap. This is what Conservation rescues you from. I wasn't being loyal to myself; I was leaking out of guilt, bargaining my health for approval that never pays back.

That's when I centered myself and remembered who I am. I remembered the truth that in silence, I build wholeness. In stepping back, I am aligned, not merely absent.

So, I left work that day. And instead of guilt, I felt reclamation. *Rest became reparations. Rest became rebellion. Rest said: "I deserve to conserve."*

Because Conservation isn't passive. It's active protection of your lifeforce. It's choosing to step back, not because you're weak, but because you know your strength isn't built by depletion. It's built by alignment.

That day, I chose to honor the quiet within me. And the world didn't end. My work didn't collapse. **What collapsed was the lie that my worth is proven by exhaustion.**

Conservation is the pause that protects your power.

It is the silence that makes space for Sovereignty.

Sacred Practice: The Fast of Noise

Choose one source of noise you feed daily (scrolling, talking, rescuing, explaining). Cut it out for 24 hours. When silence rushes in, let it speak. Write down what it says.

Sacred Rite: The Talk Fast

Anchor
We mistake noise for connection, words for worth. But silence is power. Conservation sharpens your energy and makes your presence undeniable without saying a thing.

The Rite
- Choose a block of time (starting with 1 hour) where you will not speak.
- Turn off music, background noise, and distractions.
- Move through your day in silence preparing food, journaling, walking, without words.

Integration

Notice how others respond when you don't fill the space. Notice how your body feels when you aren't translating every thought into speech. Silence isn't emptiness… it's density. It holds weight. It teaches you what really needs to be said and what was only habit.

Prompt
What truth rose up when you stopped speaking? Write it down.

Closing Affirmation (Seal)

"No one is coming to save me, and I can't save anybody. I save myself by conserving my energy, my words, and my power."

Closing Key:

Silence is not absence, its presence amplified. What you withhold strengthens what you embody.

SACRED AF

SACRED AF

CHAPTER EIGHT

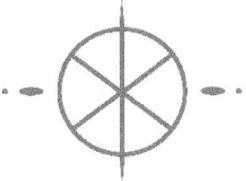

SOVEREIGNTY

*My power is not given, it is remembered.
I am the crown, the law, the throne.
Sovereignty is not earned. It is embodied in me.*

Listen: Sacred AF- Sovereignty Sound Escape (Ritual Grade Edition)

SACRED AF

Sovereignty is the rebellion of self-rule.

Sovereignty is not rebellion for rebellion's sake, nor is it a posture of defiance. It is the reclamation of your right to author your life at the deepest level: spirit, mind, body, and energy.

Most people live under the illusion of freedom. They believe they are choosing, but only from the menu handed to them: family expectations, cultural scripts, political systems, religious dogma. That's not sovereignty, that's supervised autonomy.

True sovereignty begins when you recognize you are not just a player in the game. You are the one who sets the rules of play. You are not just a vibration, you are a dimension. You don't bend to a structure, **you become the structure**.

Sovereignty demands precision with your words, because your words are law.

It demands presence, because autopilot is slavery. It demands alignment, because you cannot declare yourself sovereign while living chained to programming you never questioned.

This is why sovereignty is spiritual: it is not about overthrowing external rulers, but about de-throning the false rulers inside you—the lies, fears, and contracts you unconsciously signed. When you do, you step into the throne of your own being, and from there, everything you touch bends to your dimension. That's why sovereignty must be practiced, not posed. Presence first, then precision.

Sovereignty is not just about making choices. It's about becoming the atmosphere itself. You don't just live in reality, you radiate one. You are a walking, breathing dimension.

Think of it like this: every thought, every word, every expectation is a seed. But sovereignty is when you stop planting in someone else's garden and realize you *are* the soil. It's not a metaphor. It's physics of consciousness.

You are the frequency field. Others walk into you and feel the climate you set.

This is why sovereignty can't be outsourced. You can't "borrow" a dimension from your partner, your teacher, or a trend online. That's survival by proxy. Sovereignty is becoming your own portal, so alive in your truth that reality bends inside your orbit.

When you own your sovereignty, your presence speaks louder than any affirmation. You don't need to announce what dimension you're in. People feel it the moment they step into your field.

This is the ultimate rebellion: not just playing in the algorithm of life but becoming the algorithm itself. Not scrolling through realities but emanating one.

Sovereignty is ownership at the level of being. You are not just a body moving through space. You are space itself, coded by intention, magnetized by awareness. And once you claim that truth, you stop chasing timelines. You bend them.

This is why you can walk into a room and change the atmosphere without saying a word. Your energy field arrives before you do. People feel it before they understand it. Some are magnetized. Some are repelled. None are neutral because dimensions alter everything they touch.

Most people don't realize this, so they let their dimensions be built on autopilot. Programmed by family, culture, trauma, media, repetition. They live inside dimensions coded by fear, lack, and unworthiness. Then they wonder why the same cycles keep looping.

Here's the code: if you don't write the program of your reality, someone else already has.

You can become a dimension on purpose.

When you embody clarity, you generate a field of clarity. When you embody sovereignty, you generate a field of sovereignty. When you embody love, you generate a field of love that others step into the moment they step into *you*.

When you do this consistently, when you live so deeply in alignment that your frequency imprints on every space you enter, you stop "manifesting" and start magnetizing. You no longer chase reality. Reality bends into your dimension.

To become a dimension is to stop being only a person reacting to the world and start being a world that the universe reacts to.

Words are not suggestions.

They are contracts.

And contracts, once spoken, don't ask for clarification.

I learned this the hardest way. When my twins were born three months early and placed in the NICU, I performed a ritual. My petition was simple: "Bring them home safe and healthy." The universe answered, just not how I thought it would. Alchemy came home in a box, cremated. Khemistry came home two months later. The law was fulfilled. My words were honored. But I had not been precise in their meaning.

It happened again with a lawsuit. I asked for $15,000. I received it on paper. But after fees and costs, only $3,000 reached my hands. My words had been fulfilled. My reality, not what I intended.

Here's the code: **sovereignty with words means precision.**

Vagueness is permission for the universe to improvise. And the law will never play dumb. It only multiplies what was said, not what was secretly hoped for.

This is why your words must be sovereign. Not sloppy. Not sentimental. Not left open for interpretation. You don't say "I want more money." You say, "I call in $15,000 cleared and in my possession." You don't say "bring them home safe and healthy." You say, "I call my children home alive, thriving, and whole in my arms."

Sovereignty is realizing that your voice is a gavel. Every word you release strikes reality into form. Speak with precision or prepare to live with loopholes.

Before you speak, write, or ritualize, run it through these keys:

1. **Clarity over comfort.**
   Don't assume the universe "knows what you mean." Say it as if you're writing a legal contract.

2. **Be exact with outcomes.**
   Name the details: amount cleared and received, form of delivery, timing, state of being.

3. **Affirm life, wholeness, and thriving.**
   Don't leave your petitions half-built. Speak for the fullness of what you want, not just the outline.

4. **Avoid vagueness.**
   "More" money, "better" health, "safer" love…all of these leave room for loopholes. Anchor specifics.

5. **Close the back door.**
   Add a line of sovereignty: *"This or greater, in alignment with my highest good, now."* That way nothing can slip in sideways.

There's a line you have to draw in sovereignty, and you must ask yourself: *Are you covering your loved ones in love, or are you trying to control their outcomes?*

Covering is frequency. It's radiance.

When you hold someone in love, you extend your field without crossing their will. You become a shelter they can step into if they choose. You're not bending reality *for them*; you're emanating a vibration they can align with.

Imposing, on the other hand, will dress up as love. It says, "I know what's best for you, so let me rewrite your story." That's not sovereignty, that's interference. **The law doesn't bless interference.**

When I covered my twins, I thought I was protecting them. But in truth, I was trying to control the outcome instead of anchoring in the frequency of life, wholeness, and thriving.

My default is to fix. Fix people, fix situations, fix things. I've built a life around solving, troubleshooting, adjusting what's broken.

I work in customer service, which means forty hours a week of carrying other people's fires until they're extinguished. When I clock out, I don't want to be anyone's savior. I'm emptied out. I'm honest about the capacity I have, and yet **honesty gets mistaken for disregard.**

That's not disregard.
That's survival.

Empathy exhaustion is real. Sovereignty requires you to admit it. Because the trap of fixing is just another way of imposing your will on someone else's dimension.

You cannot save people by stripping them of their power.

When you move like that, you're not healing, you're interfering. You're trying to bend their story to your script, instead of letting them author their own. And that's the shadow side of compassion: it becomes control dressed in kindness.

Sovereignty interrupts this cycle. It teaches you that silence is not neglect. Restraint is not cruelty. Sometimes the most loving act is to let someone stumble in their own dimension until they decide to rise.

Sovereignty requires that you release control while holding love.

Your word creates your dimension. Their words create theirs. The only field you truly command is your own. The question isn't: "Can I cover them?" It's: "Can I stand so fully in love, wholeness, and alignment that they feel safe to step into my dimension, without me scripting their fate?"

When you step outside of dysfunction, you see it everywhere. And once you've tasted sovereignty, the dysfunction doesn't just feel uncomfortable. It feels unlivable.

That's when the isolation comes. Not because you want to be alone, but because **you realize how much energy it takes to stay in spaces that feed on your light without ever fueling it.**

I feel everything. I see everything. I don't miss much, and sometimes that feels like a curse. The static of unhealed people and unhealed places weighs heavy, and if I stay too long, I start to mistake their noise for my own. So, I cocoon. Not to hide, but to protect my field. To let my nervous system breathe.

But here's the thing about cocooning: you can't stay wrapped up forever. Eventually, wings demand flight. And when you emerge, the hardest part isn't flying… it's choosing where to fly.

I wanted to soar in front of the people I loved most, but my soaring wasn't normal to them. They didn't know what to do with it. The words were there, but the investment wasn't. That's the cost of soaring:

it exposes who can only celebrate you in theory and who will actually invest in your becoming.

Cocooning is not weakness. It's necessary to rest. Flying is not egotistical. It's inevitable truth. The wisdom is in where you open your wings and in knowing that support has frequency too.

Sovereignty means accepting that not everyone will understand your flight. But those who do? They'll catch the wind beneath you.

It is in this space and time that judgment will serve your becoming. It's important to know that judgment is not the enemy. You cannot walk in sovereignty without judgment, because judgment is simply discernment. It's the ability to see clearly what belongs in your field and what doesn't.

Judgment is the ability to assess situations, people, environments with clarity of mind. It names reality.

Judgment has been demonized and confused with the frequency of condemnation. Condemnation is judgment weaponized. It doesn't just name what it is; it fixates, condemns, and binds you to the very thing you've outgrown. Sovereignty demands the courage to discern without the compulsion to condemn.

The temptation comes when judgment calcifies into condemnation. Judgment says: *This is not for me.* Condemnation says: *This is not for anyone.* Judgment directs you back to your path. Condemnation tries to erase theirs.

And here's the line most people miss: when you condemn, you cross the boundary of sovereignty. Because condemnation is not just discernment, it's control. It's an attempt to impose your will on someone else's dimension, to declare their becoming invalid because it doesn't look like yours.

That's not sovereignty. That's empire. And empire is always unsustainable, because it requires invasion to stay alive.

Sovereignty doesn't need to rewrite anyone else's story. It doesn't need to sentence, to punish, to erase. It simply rules its own domain with such clarity that interference becomes unnecessary.

That's sovereignty.

Anything else is just control in disguise.

Sacred Practice: Throne Check

Look at one area where you've handed your power to someone else: their opinion, their approval, their validation. Reclaim it by writing one sentence: *"I rule here."* Say it out loud three times. Feel it settle.

Sacred Rite: Claim Your Power

- Find a mirror and stand tall in front of it.
- Place your hands gently on your head as if crowning yourself.
- Look yourself in the eyes and speak one decree that defines your authority (ex: "I decide who I am." "I choose my path." "My will is sacred.").
- Say it three times: once soft, once steady, once with full power.
- Lower your hands to your heart and finish with: *"I rule me."*

Anchor:
Every yes is a spell. Every no is a shield. Sovereignty is the art of choosing from alignment rather than fear. This rite aligns your will with your becoming.

The Rite:
- Write down three areas in your life where you feel stuck.
- For each, ask: *"If I chose from alignment, not fear, what would my yes be?"*

- Circle the one that feels most urgent. Take one step toward it within 24 hours.

Integration:
Every time you practice the Aligned Yes, you fortify your sovereignty. Fear shrinks. Alignment expands.

Reflection Prompt:
Which yes felt most powerful? What action did you take to honor it?

Closing Affirmation (Seal)

"I am sovereign. My choices are my crown. My will shapes my world."

Closing Key:
"Power is not given, it is remembered. I rule because I am."

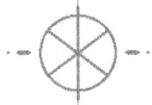

SACRED AF

SACRED AF

CHAPTER NINE

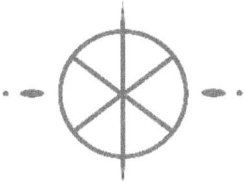

ENERGY CLEARING

*My release is not loss. My release is return.
Every cord I cut, every residue I burn, is my declaration:
I come back to myself whole.*

Listen: Sacred AF- Energy Clearing Sound Escape (Ritual Grade Edition)

SACRED AF

We've now arrived at the final key, and it carries the frequency of 9: endings, completion, sacred subtraction. It is not what you expect.

This chapter is not about smudging, crystal grids, singing bowls, spiritual baths, or incense. Those are tools, not truth. I could list them, but where's the revolution in that?

Energy clearing cannot be outsourced to shamans, healers, or rituals. It is not optional; it is the core of sovereignty. **The energy you've accumulated is yours to clear.** Your code has been corrupted, and it is your responsibility to debug your own operating system.

Clearing is not external. It is internal.

Through each initiation, you've dug deep and rewritten your code. Now it is time to reset the frequency. And to reset, you must release. You must return to nothing. Because only from nothing does something new emerge. Nothing comes through a closed fist. You have to let go to hold space for what you are magnetizing.

Make no mistake: every interaction leaves a trace. Every expectation, every argument, every wound lingers like static in your field until you decide to clear it. Without release, you become a house overrun with clutter: crowded, heavy, unlivable.

Clearing is not a luxury ritual. It is daily maintenance for the soul. Just as you wash your body, you must also wash your energy. Otherwise, you will carry what is not yours and mistake it for identity.

This is where the distinction matters: transformation is rebirth; clearing is maintenance.

Transformation burns everything down so something new can emerge. Clearing keeps your field clean, so you don't mistake yesterday's debris for today's self. Transformation without clearing leaves residue. Clearing without transformation just rearranges the clutter. You need both but you must know which one you are in.

But the world trains you to accumulate. To hoard more, to chase more, to define yourself by how much you can stack – things, titles, roles. It calls that life. But becoming is not just about what you add. It is about what you are willing to release.

Energy clearing is the rebellion of subtraction.

It is the courage to choose death. The death of versions of yourself that cannot walk with you where you are going.

I once pursued a leadership position I thought I wanted. When it didn't open up in my timing, I surrendered. I released the attachment, and almost as if on cue, the opportunity came back around. Two rounds of interviews in, I realized the position fit who I used to be, not who I was becoming.

So, I withdrew myself from consideration for the position.

In that moment, I took my power back through release. As much as they were interviewing me, I was interviewing them. I wasn't negotiating from scarcity, but from abundance. I was already at peace in my current role, so the only thing that promotion could have given me was a title, pseudo-freedom, and a cage disguised as more money. That was a price I refused to pay.

This is energy clearing. **Letting go of what doesn't fit** even when it looks shiny, even when it's hard to walk away. Because if it doesn't match your becoming, it will drain you. Clearing creates space. And space is where sovereignty breathes.

The scariest death you will ever face is not physical. It is the death of identities. The death of who you thought you were. The death of contracts you never consciously signed.

Every clearing is a funeral. Not for your body, but for your illusions.

Residue collects in layers:
- **Emotional residue** is the grief, shame, anger, and regret left behind by unprocessed moments.
- **Relational residue** is the attachments, obligations, and scripts from others you still carry long after they've left the room.
- **Ancestral residue** is the weight of inherited contracts, silences, and generational wounds coded into your lineage.

You don't dissolve residue by ignoring it. You dissolve it by naming it, facing it, and refusing to carry it as identity.

This is where grief becomes holy. Transformation showed you grief as fire, as paradox, as burning and becoming. Energy clearing shows you grief as reverence.

Grief is proof that something mattered. That you loved. That you were alive enough to be moved. To clear grief is not to discard it, but to honor it. To say: *thank you for what you gave me. Thank you for shaping me. Now I release you with dignity.*

Without reverence, clearing becomes violence. With reverence, clearing becomes sacred subtraction.

Grief is the highest form of clearing. Not weakness. Not collapse. But reverence.

To grieve is to bow to what once held meaning. To give thanks for what once carried you. To hold a sacred funeral for an identity, a season, a relationship, or a dream that no longer walks with you into the future.

Most people skip grief. They discard without honoring. They run toward distraction instead of reverence. But sovereign grief is holy. It does not discard. It sanctifies.

Sovereign grief says: I honor what was, and because I honor it, I now release it.

It creates a portal for the next chapter by closing the last one with gratitude. This is why grief is not just emotional; it is spiritual technology. It clears static. It severs cords. It unclutters the field so your frequency can reset. Grief is not absence. It is sacred space.

There are also energies that create residue in the soul. The residue can linger long after the moment has passed:

- **Disappointment** is the ghost of unmet expectations.
- **Shame** whispers that you *are* wrong, not just that you did wrong.
- **Blame** locks you in a courtroom of unfinished trials.
- **Guilt** masquerades as responsibility but is really self-punishment in disguise.

These *squatters of the soul* are trapped until released. The danger isn't just in feeling them. The danger is in rehearsing them until they calcify into identity. You stop saying, "I feel guilty," and start believing, "I *am* guilt."

Energy clearing refuses that lie. You are not your disappointments. You are not your shame. You are not your guilt or your blame. These are not essence. They are residue.

The rebel move is to clear them. To feel them fully, honor the lesson, and then release them before they root into your becoming.

Clearing does not erase. It transforms.

It says: *I honor what this showed me. And now, I let it go.*

The same is true for soul ties and attachments. Not every bond needs to be severed with rage. Some need to be released with gratitude, even if they have caused pain.
Ties are proof that something once touched you. Clearing does not erase the bond; it frees you from its grip. Reverence closes the loop, so you do not repeat the cycle.

This is where the Taoist essence of non-ado speaks: you do not clear to get an outcome, or to control what happens after. You clear because clearing itself is holy. You act, not as a bargain, but as alignment with the natural rhythm of endings. To release without agenda is the deepest freedom.

Clearing also restores your energy economy. Every tie, every residue, every illusion carried is a debt against your lifeforce. Clearing resets you to liquidity. It frees the bandwidth you need to build. Without clearing, you are forever overdrawn. With clearing, you step into surplus.

This is why embracing the Law of Surrender can be challenging. To surrender is not weakness. It is the deliberate act of release. It is dropping your compulsion to control outcomes. It is trading perfection for excellence, because excellence is the highest we can command with clarity and discipline.

Surrender is trusting the empty space.

To clear is to honor endings. To cut cords. To cleanse your space. To reclaim your breath, your body, your field. Energy clearing is rebellion against energetic colonization. It is saying: **my field belongs to me.**

And when you reclaim your field, you step lighter. Freer. Unburdened.

Obsession with clearing can become another leak. Some people turn it into performance; endless rituals, constant cord-cutting, perpetual "releasing" without ever building anything new. That is not sovereignty. That is avoidance dressed up as spirituality. Clearing is meant to create space for becoming, not keep you in a cycle of perpetual subtraction.

Indeed, clearing feels like loss, but it is actually liberation. Completion is not a void; it is an opening. Endings are not absence, they are portals.

To clear is to complete. To complete is to rise.

Sacred Practice: Cut & Return

Notice one place where your energy feels tangled: a draining person, a looping memory, a toxic belief. Close your eyes and make a cutting motion with your hand as you say: *"I return this. I return to me."* Then do a simple cleanse: water, smoke, or even shake it off.

Sacred Rite: Cord Cut & Cleanse

Anchor:
Not everything you carry is yours. Energy accumulates other people's emotions, ancestral weight, and energetic residue. This rite releases what is not yours and returns you to yourself.

The Rite:
- Close your eyes. Visualize cords stretching from your body to people, places, or beliefs that drain you.
- With your hand, make a cutting motion across your body and say: *"I release what is not mine."*
- Follow with a physical cleanse: shower, smoke cleanse, salt bath,

or shaking your body out.
- Seal it by saying: *"I return to me, whole and clear."*

Integration:
Repeat this rite whenever you feel heavy with what doesn't belong to you. Release is holy.

Reflection Prompt:
What cords did you cut today? How did your body respond once they were gone?

Closing Affirmation (Seal)

"I let go of what is not mine. In release, I reclaim my field, my freedom, my wholeness."

Closing Key

Clearing is not loss- it is sovereignty restored.

SACRED AF

THE FINAL RITE OF BECOMING

You don't need more steps. You don't need more teachers. You don't need more proof.

You've walked through the keys. You've seen yourself in the fire and in the silence. You've been handed language for truths you already carried.

Now comes the only part that matters: living it.

Sacred AF was never about information. It was about initiation. Every word here was a mirror, not a map. The map is already inside you. The law is already in your breath.

This is the seal:

My becoming is not pending. It is now.

Say it. Mean it. Move in it.

Because there is no other rite, no other ritual, no other rebellion greater than this... to live your life unapologetically authored, sovereign in your truth, unafraid of your own power.

Go live it raw. Go live it sacred... AS FUCK.

SACRED AF

EPILOGUE: THE WAY FORWARD

You have crossed the threshold. The nine keys have done their work, and the final rite has sealed your becoming. But this is not an ending. It is a continuation.

Every choice you make from this moment forward is part of your practice. Every breath, every "Yes," every "No," is a thread you weave into the tapestry of your life. You are the artist and the architect. You are the ritual and the result.

Becoming is a spiral, not a straight line. You will return to these keys again, and each time they will meet you at a new depth. They will not read the same twice—because you will not be the same reader twice.
Carry these pages not as rules, but as reminders. Return when you forget. Add your own rites. Rewrite your own affirmations. Make the journey yours.

Above all—remember you are not lost.

You are the blueprint. You are the becoming.

And so, it is.

For more resources, visit https://oraclekeys.com/sacredaf/.

SACRED AF

ABOUT THE AUTHOR

Oracle Keys is a writer and visionary devoted to language as living technology, using words that awaken, disrupt, and return the reader to themselves. A modern mystic with a rebel's precision, this work speaks to those dismantling performance and remembering truth.

Her writing explores the intersections of discipline, sovereignty, and self-remembrance. Every sentence is built as architecture for becoming, designed to confront programming, fracture illusion, and reassemble power from within.

Each text functions as a mirror rather than a map, an invitation to experience transformation as an act of remembrance. The work itself is the ritual.

The name *Oracle Keys* is not a mask but a vessel. There is no persona to follow, only transmissions to encounter. What endures is not the author, but the frequency.

SACRED AF

NOTES & REFLECTIONS

SACRED AF

SACRED AF

SACRED AF

SACRED AF

SACRED AF

www.ingramcontent.com/pod-product-compliance
Lightning Source LLC
Chambersburg PA
CBHW051132160426
43195CB00014B/2448